AN EXTRAORDINARY EXPERIENCE
Prophet Muhammad for Little Hearts

by

S Khan

Goodword**kidz**

Helping you build a family of faith

One night, as the Prophet Muhammad ﷺ slept
next to the Kabah, the Archangel Jibril woke
him and took him on a strange, white winged
animal, called Buraq (lightning),

3

from Makkah to al-Aqsa mosque in far away Jerusalem. There the Prophet Muhammad ﷺ met Ibrahim عليه السلام, Musa عليه السلام and Isa عليه السلام and the other prophets, and they prayed together.

Then Jibril took the Prophet ﷺ through Heaven's gates, where he saw countless angels.

One was Malik the Keeper of hell, who never smiles. Malik gave the Prophet a glimpse into Hell to let him see the misery of those who suffered there. The angels then took the Prophet ﷺ through the Seven Heavens, one by one.

Beyond the seventh heaven, the Prophet ﷺ passed through the veils covering that which is hidden, until at last he came into the divine Light of Allah's Presence. The Prophet ﷺ looked upon that which the eyes cannot see and minds cannot imagine, the Creator of the heavens and the earth. Time, thought and feelings vanished; there was only great peace and the brilliance of pure light.

11

Too soon, the experience ended and he was brought back
to earth. The Prophet ﷺ was amazed to find the spot
where he had lain was still warm, and the cup he had
tipped over was still emptying. This incredible experience
had taken place in less than a moment!

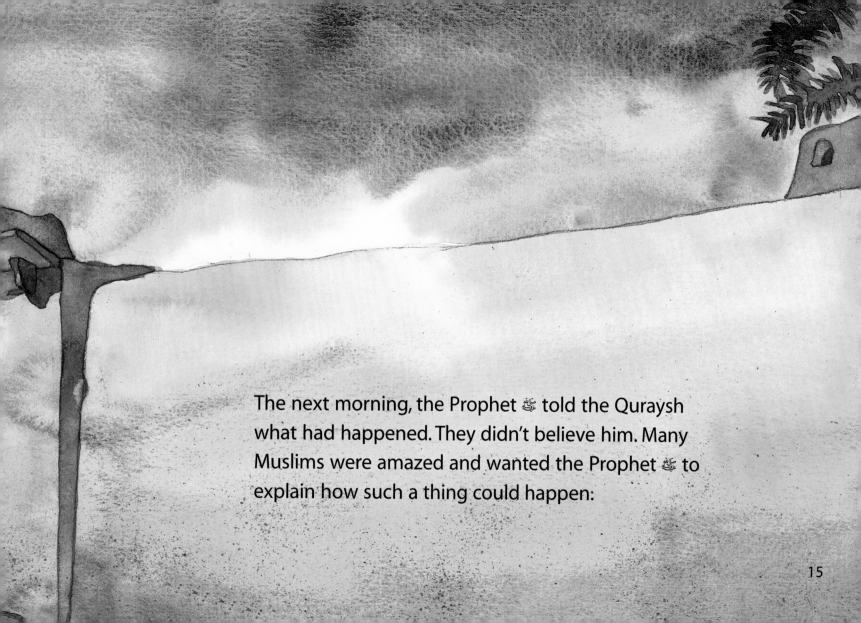

The next morning, the Prophet ﷺ told the Quraysh what had happened. They didn't believe him. Many Muslims were amazed and wanted the Prophet ﷺ to explain how such a thing could happen:

But the Prophet's description of Jerusalem, and the caravans he had seen on the way back to Makkah, convinced them he was telling the truth.

It was during this experience that Allah's commandment on prayer was revealed to the Prophet Muhammad ﷺ. He reported that Allah wanted men to pray fifty times a day, but that on the Prophet Musa's advice, he had appealed for a less difficult routine. At last Allah resolved that there should be five prayers a day. That has remained Muslim practice ever since.

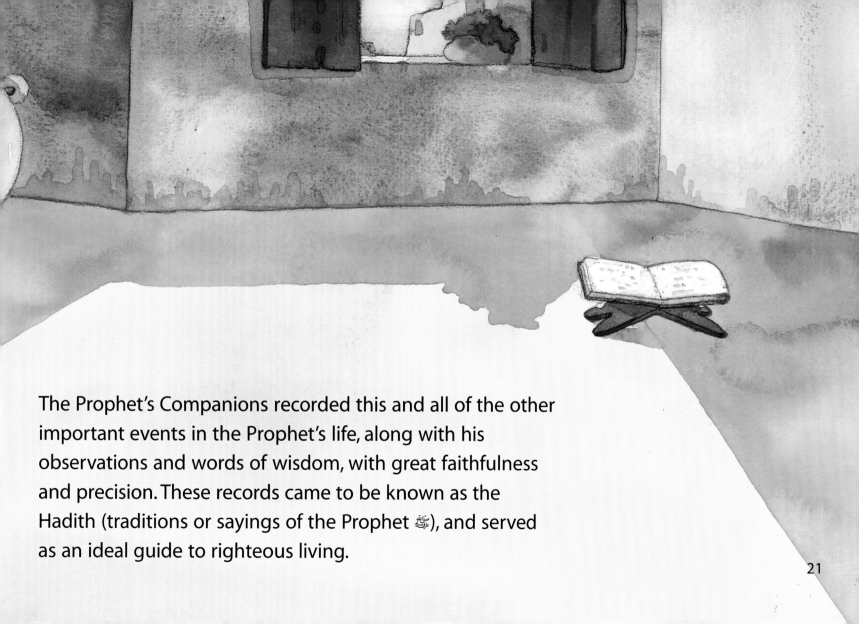

The Prophet's Companions recorded this and all of the other important events in the Prophet's life, along with his observations and words of wisdom, with great faithfulness and precision. These records came to be known as the Hadith (traditions or sayings of the Prophet ﷺ), and served as an ideal guide to righteous living.

One collector of Hadith stands out from the others. He was a cousin of the Prophet ﷺ, by the name of 'Abdullah ibn 'Abbas. He was only thirteen when the Prophet died. It is said that he memorized no less than 1660 sayings of the Prophet ﷺ, and would go to as many as thirty Companions to make sure that his version of each *hadith* was correct. Once, when he went to check on a *hadith* previously unknown to him, he found the Companion having his afternoon nap. Not wishing to disturb him, he waited outside in the heat and dust. When the Companion came out, he said: "O cousin of the Prophet ﷺ! What is the matter with you? If you had sent for me, I would have come to you." "I am the one who should come to you," replied 'Abdullah, "for knowledge is sought—it does not just come."

23

For the Prophet ﷺ, the Night Journey and the Ascension was a turning point. After years of persecution and the terrible sadness of losing both Khadijah and Abu Talib, the experience gave him great comfort and the strength to go on. He became convinced that Allah was always with him.